AF291878

The Return of the Native
Suky Best

Film and Video Umbrella

Introduction
Steven Bode

This publication records a new, and especially haunting, body of work by the artist, Suky Best. Continuing her long-standing fascination with wildlife and its various contemporary and art-historical representations, *The Return of the Native* is a series of photographs and short video animations that highlights the steady decline and, in some cases, all-too-sudden disappearance of once-familiar species of animal, insect and bird life from large swathes of the English landscape.

The series consists of two separate sets of commissions. The first, produced by Film and Video Umbrella and Norwich School of Art and Design for a three-year programme of artists' projects entitled 'Silicon Fen', is sited among the distinctive horizons of the East Anglian Fenland; formerly desolate and remote, now extensively, and intensively, farmed. The second, produced by Film and Video Umbrella and Pump House Gallery for an expanded version of *The Return of the Native* at their exhibition space in Battersea Park in London, homes in on the modern metropolis and the threat posed to the city's fragile patches of wildlife by increased urban development.

The story is the same in both places, as it is throughout much of the rest of England — a sharp, and accelerating, fall-off in both the variety and the numbers of species, with scores of previously common birds and insects, including some particularly cherished and iconic examples, now either endangered or extinct.

With specimens sourced from local museums, and using simple digital techniques to superimpose them onto the backdrop of each miniature landscape, Best 'reintroduces' a number of formerly indigenous species into habitats where they are now seldom or no longer seen. The slightly studied and stylised nature of her compositions, in which the respective elements somehow don't quite fit together, underlines the ghostly, apparitional character of each encounter, instilling a feeling of disquiet about the changes we are making to our natural environment and acting as a vivid reminder of what we have already, irretrievably, lost.

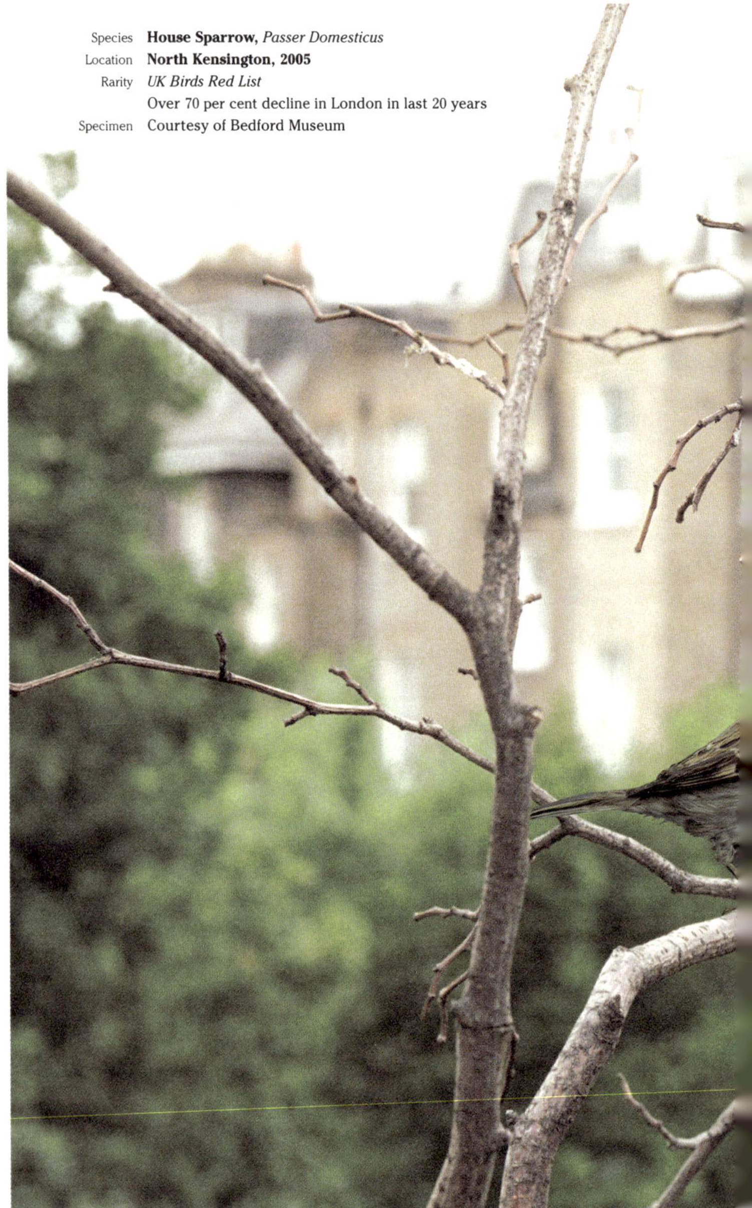

Species   House Sparrow, Passer Domesticus
Location North Kensington, 2005
Rarity   UK Birds Red List
          Over 70 per cent decline in London in last 20 years
Specimen Courtesy of Bedford Museum

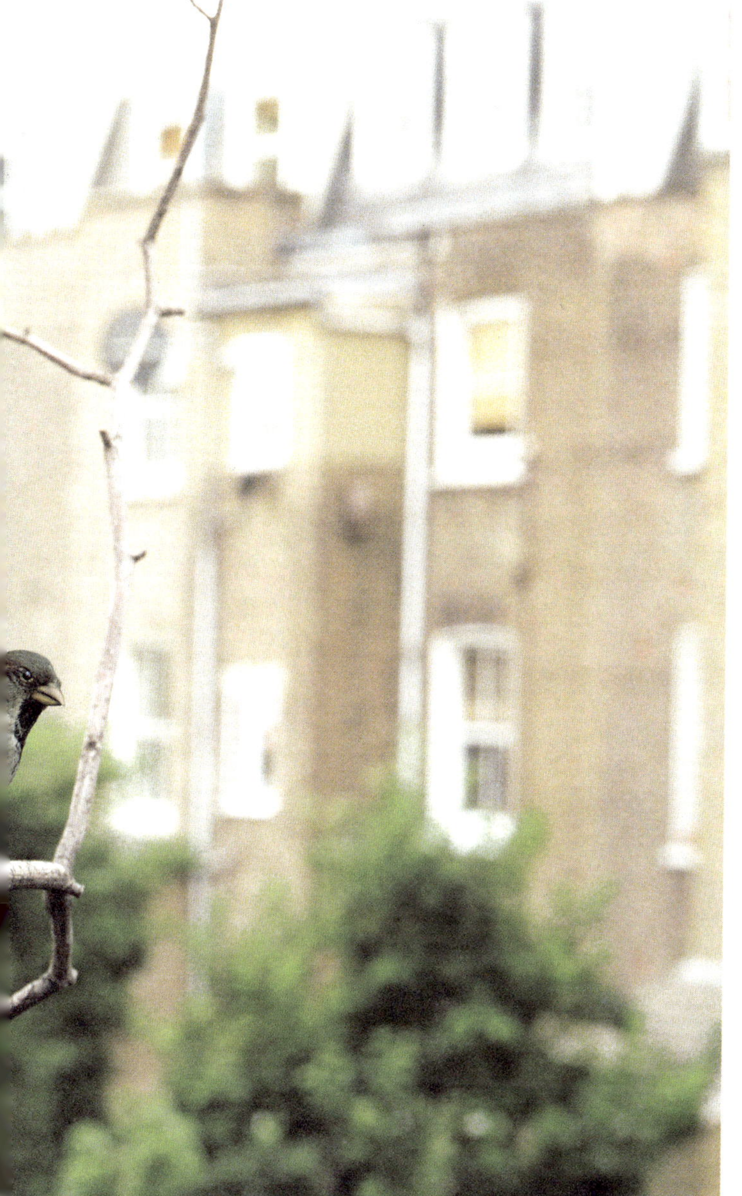

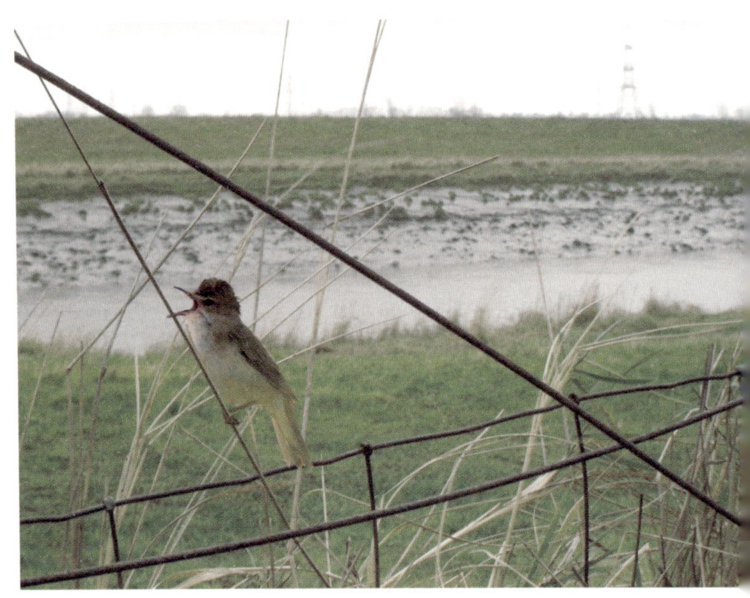

Species	**Marsh Warbler** *Acrocephalus Palustris*
Location	**Near Sutton Bridge, 2005**
Rarity	*UK Birds Red List*
	Never abundant, was regular Fen migrant until early 20th century
Specimen image	Courtesy of Alan Tate

The Return of the Native…
Stephen Moss

Wandering by the river's edge
I love to rustle through the sedge
And through the woods of reed to tear
Almost as high as bushes are…

In his poem 'The Fens', written almost two hundred years ago, the poet and naturalist John Clare portrayed a vanishing landscape; already disappearing as this vast region – half water, half land – was drained and ploughed in the name of Progress. Today, much of the East Anglian Fens has been further transformed into something approximating an agricultural factory, with only a straggling hedgerow or stagnant dyke a reminder of the riches the area once held.

Since Clare wandered this bleak, yet strangely magical landscape, observing the comings and goings of wild creatures, the natural history of the Fens has been a story of decline, and in some cases extinction. Locations that once rang to the metallic call of Bearded Tits, or the buzzing of bumblebees, are now silent; the natural sounds replaced by the monotonous drone of the combine harvester. Plants such as the Fen Violet and Fen Orchid are confined to the tiny patches salvaged as nature reserves; while the insects that depended on the rich local flora are either extinct or reduced to a remnant population, clinging to a precarious existence.

Amongst the first species to disappear, over 150 years ago, was the Large Copper Butterfly — one of the most beautiful of all our native species. Rare and localised, and living on the very northern edge of its range, the Large Copper was always at risk; the early destruction of its wetland habitat was the final nail in the coffin. Others, like the Short-tailed Bumblebee (finally declared extinct in the mid 1990s), hung on almost to the present day, but finally succumbed to the inexorable spread of farms, roads and housing. The visitor to what passes today for 'Fenland' can only guess at the wealth of wildlife this area must once have supported, as they listen to a solitary Skylark trying to be heard above the noise of traffic and farm machinery.

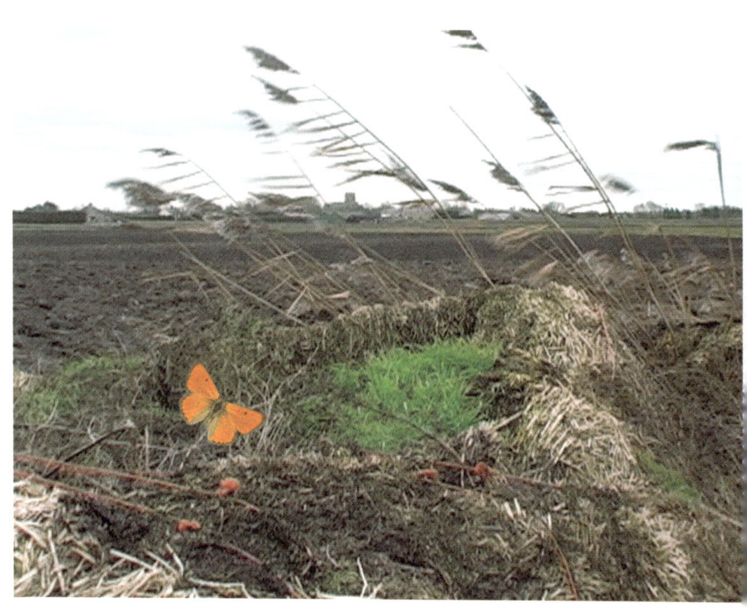

Species **Large Copper Butterfly,** *Lycaena Dispar*
Location **Near Ramsey, 2005**
Rarity *Extinct* UK, 1864
Last seen Fens, 1851
IUCN globally threatened species
Specimen Courtesy of Bedford Museum

The urban jungle of Britain's capital city could hardly be further removed from the bleak, open landscape of the Fens. Yet the changing face, and fate, of London's wildlife has much in common with that of Fenland. As the urban sprawl has spread, many wild creatures simply have not been able to cope, and have either declined or become extinct.

Some species were never going to survive in the modern city. The Greater Horseshoe Bat, one of our largest species, has declined by 98 per cent in the past hundred years, and is now confined to a dozen colonies, all in south-west Britain. It is hardly surprising that the last London record was over half a century ago, in 1953. The Nightingale is faring a little better nationally, but is now rarely heard in the capital, and no longer breeds there.

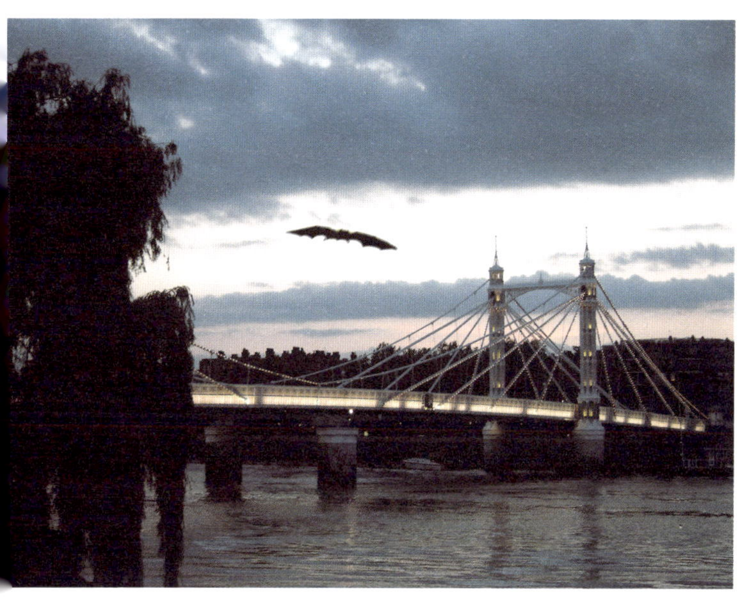

Other vulnerable species are clinging on in the oases provided by London's parks and gardens. The Stag Beetle suffers from the modern desire to tidy up woodlands, removing the dead timber crucial to its life-cycle. Ironically, London is now the number one county for this magnificent insect, though even here it is under threat from its two main predators, the Magpie and domestic cat. London is also the stronghold for the Black Redstart, a modest and often overlooked little bird. This species initially colonised London following the Second World War, taking advantage of the bomb-sites that mimicked its natural habitat of rocky mountain-sides. With these long since developed, it has switched its preference to London landmarks such as Canary Wharf and the Millennium Dome.

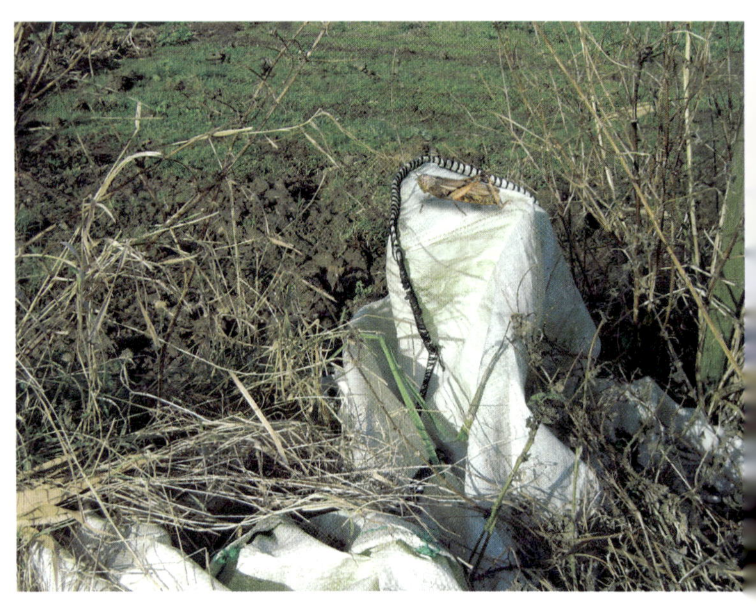

Species   **Large Marsh Grasshopper,** *Stethophyma Grossum*
Location   **Wisbeach St Mary, 2005**
Rarity   *RDB2 Vulnerable*
Last seen Wicken Fen, 1938
Restricted to Southern England
Specimen   Courtesy of Bedford Museum

On the other hand, House Sparrows, once so common and synonymous with London that the words 'me old cock sparrer' were a Cockney term of endearment, have virtually disappeared from great swathes of the city. A few remain at scattered sites such as London Zoo and the Tower; elsewhere they have vanished completely. The cause of this rapid and sudden drop in numbers remains a mystery: with mobile phone masts, chemicals in unleaded petrol and the lack of suitable nesting sites in modern buildings all implicated. Whatever the reason, the catastrophic population crash of one of our commonest city birds must surely make us stop and wonder what we have done to our urban environment.

So even though the Fens and London may not appear to have very

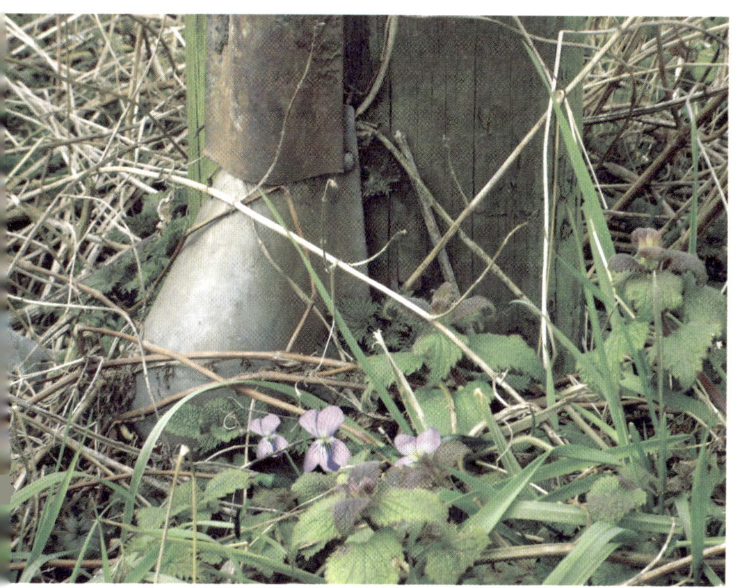

much in common, the process of decline and impoverishment in their wildlife has been strikingly similar. And this process has been mirrored throughout Britain: in woodland and farmland, heaths and downs, mountains and valleys, moors and the coast. Not every species has declined; but the pattern of slow degradation, beginning with the Industrial Revolution and accelerating apace in the sixty years since the end of the Second World War, has been remarkably similar everywhere.

A random selection of casualties includes the Red-backed Shrike, Large Blue Butterfly and Norfolk Damselfly — all now lost as British breeding species, although there are currently attempts to reintroduce the Large Blue. Other, more familiar, species have appeared on the official 'Red Data' list of conservation concern:

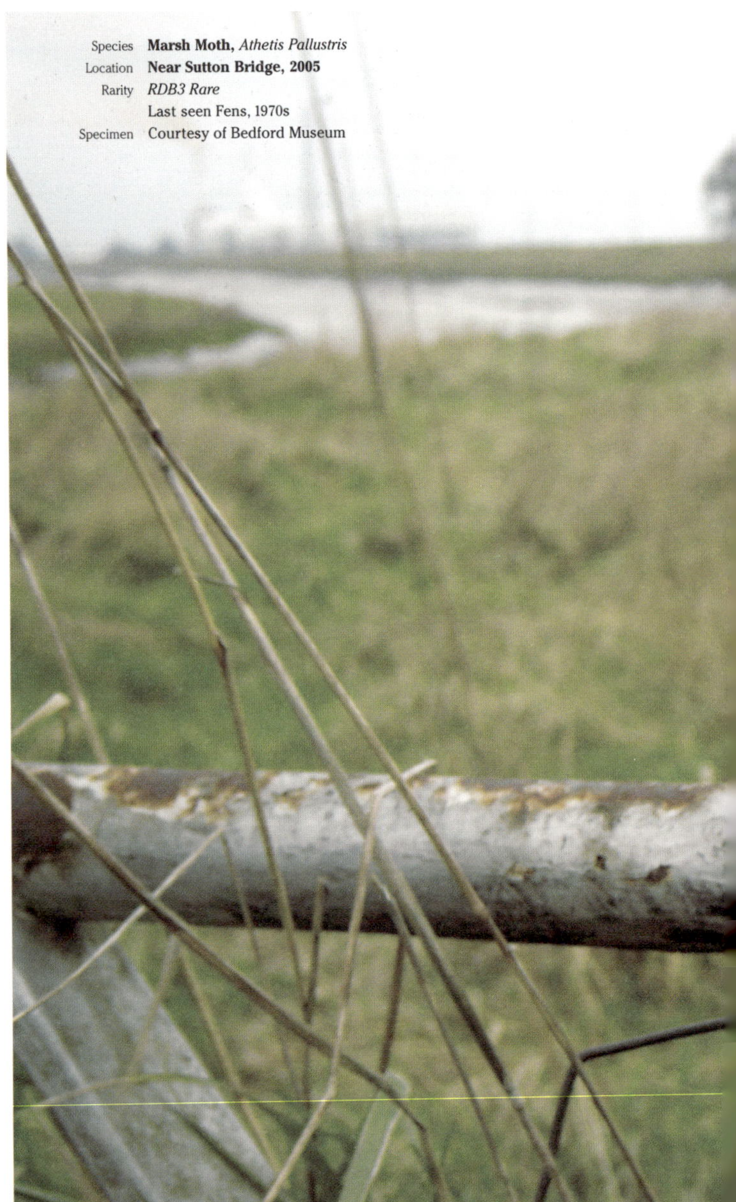

Species   **Marsh Moth,** *Athetis Pallustris*
Location   **Near Sutton Bridge, 2005**
Rarity   *RDB3 Rare*
Last seen Fens, 1970s
Specimen   Courtesy of Bedford Museum

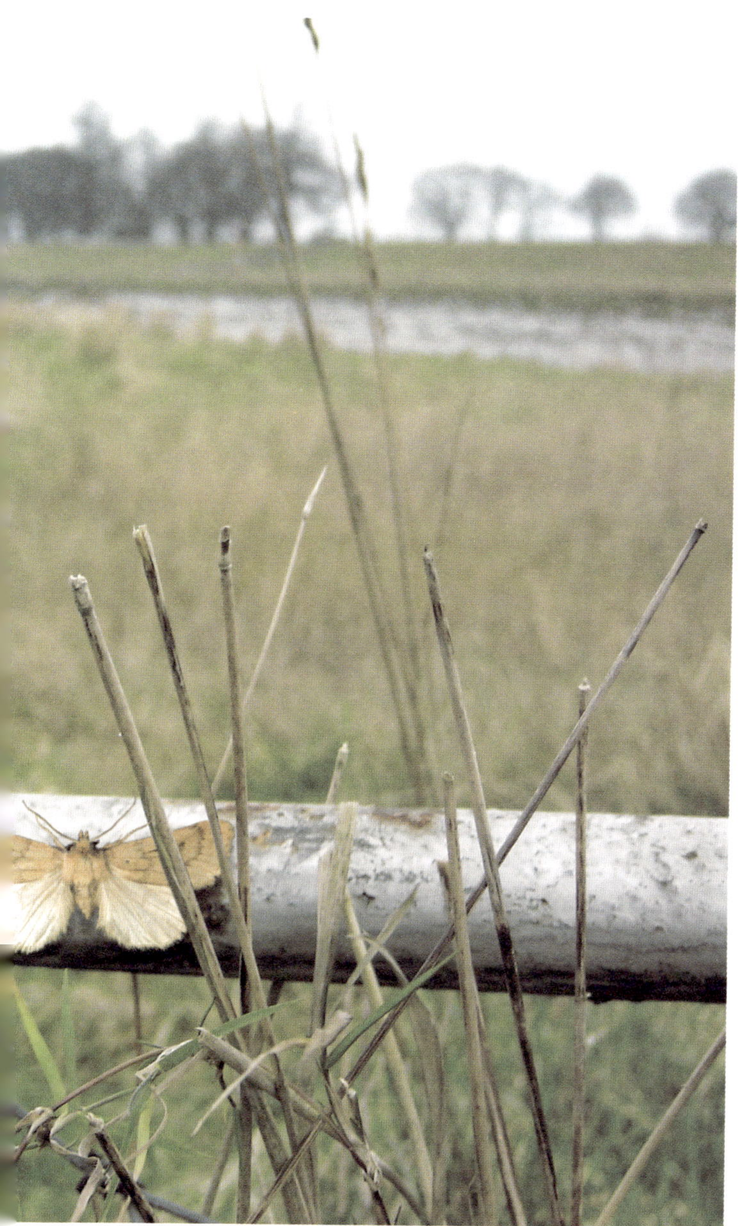

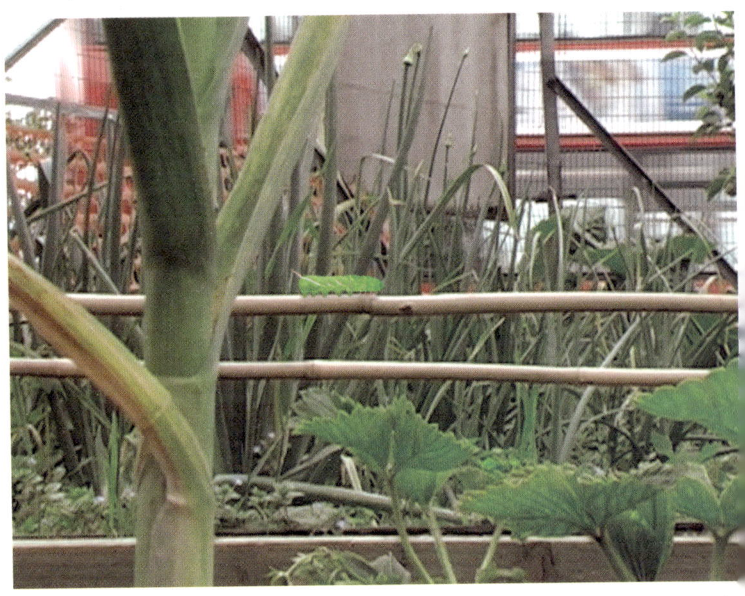

Species **Privet Hawk Moth Larva,** *Sphinx Ligustri*
Location **Bermondsey, 2005**
Rarity Previously common, London population now in decline
Depletion due mainly to loss of garden hedges
Specimen images Courtesy of Paul Chesterfield and Jayne Herbert, Cornwall Wildlife

including the Grey Partridge, Skylark and even the familiar Song Thrush. One of the problems of these declines is that we do not fully understand the reasons behind them; all we know is that if just one species disappears, the knock-on effects can be catastrophic, as the complex and intricate web of interdependency collapses before our eyes.

But to play devil's advocate for a moment, why does it matter that some creatures have declined — even to the point of extinction? After all, other species are thriving — with urban foxes and roof-nesting gulls augmented by exotic invaders such as Rose-ringed Parakeets, now a regular sight in the London suburbs.

A fall in 'biodiversity' is often cited as one reason to try to halt the declines. But nowadays naturalists are beginning to realise

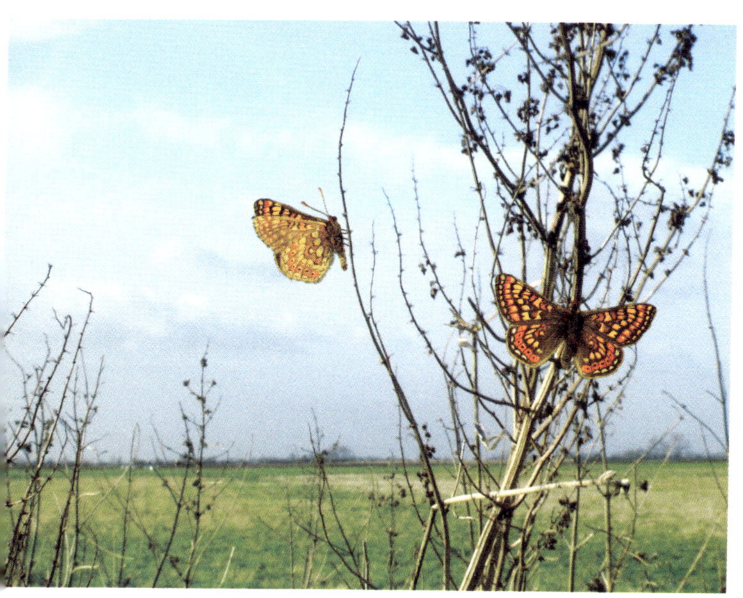

that we do not simply save species for their own sake; or just to maintain the variety and richness of our fauna and flora. Instead, we now understand that just as, in John Donne's words, 'any man's death diminishes me', so the decline or disappearance of any wild creature in some way diminishes our own relationship with Nature.

Just as many of our native species are going into freefall, the way in which we experience the natural world is also changing. Whereas once children grew up discovering nature for themselves, by gradually exploring their surroundings, nature increasingly has become just another 'leisure experience'. Nature tables in schools have disappeared on largely spurious grounds of health and safety, while pre-teenage children have had their freedom to wander

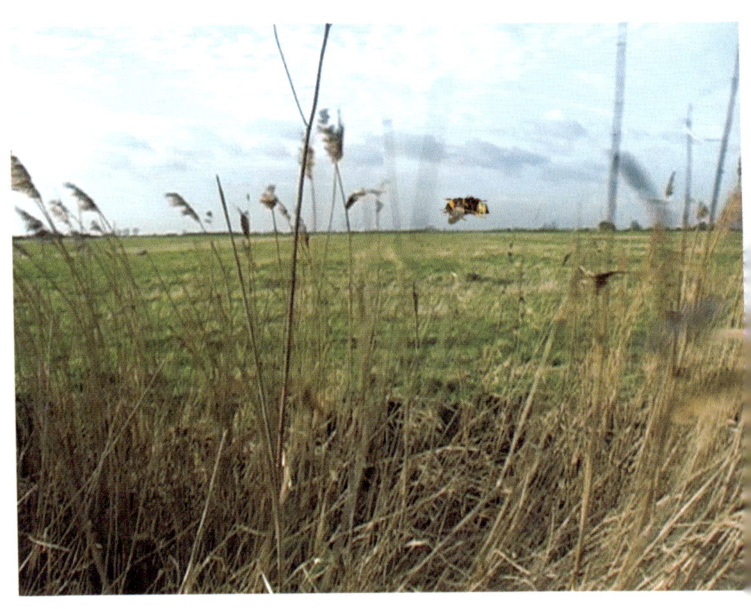

Species **Short-haired Bumblebee,** *Bombus Subterraneus*
Location **Sutton St Edmund, 2005**
Rarity *Extinct* UK, 1996
Specimen Courtesy of Bedford Museum

about on their own taken away; and replaced by organised trips to museums, exhibitions and nature reserves. Even when they do encounter wild nature, this is invariably mediated by a teacher, guide, or audio-visual aid, creating – albeit unintentionally – a barrier between the child and the wild creature or landscape they are encountering.

At home, we all have greater access to wildlife than ever before: via a computer or television screen. While the increase in television programmes about British wildlife is welcome, the experience it gives is still essentially a vicarious one. There is always the danger that having watched Bill Oddie or Alan Titchmarsh out and about looking at wildlife, viewers will have had their own desire satisfied. A more optimistic view is that the number of armchair enthusiast

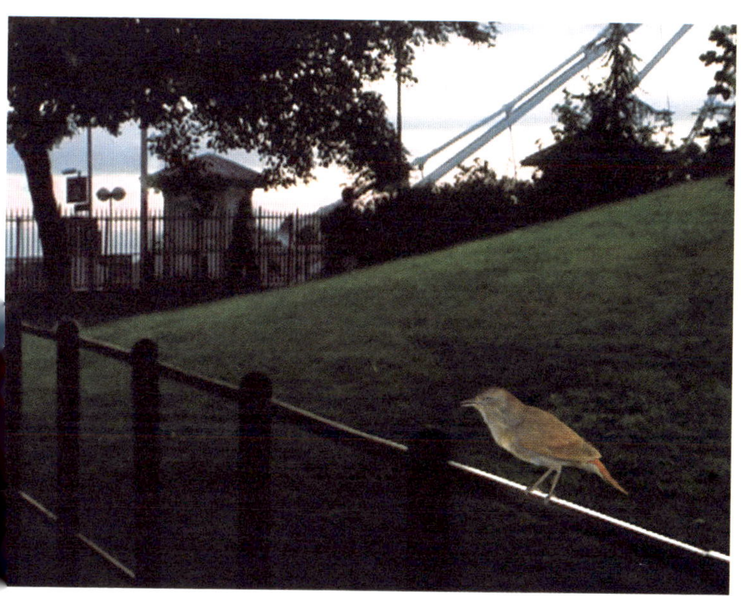

Species **Nightingale,** *Luscinia Megarhynchos*
Location **Battersea Park, 2005**
Rarity *UK Birds Amber List*
Declining throughout UK
Recorded in Central London until mid 19th century
Specimen Courtesy of Bedford Museum

will be outweighed by those stimulated to go out in the field and experience Britain's wildlife first-hand.

Nowadays many people venturing into the countryside seem to feel the need to have some purpose in mind: birdwatching, rambling or capturing the landscape in watercolours or oils. Nothing wrong with that, but how many people now just 'go for a walk', allowing themselves to experience nature in the raw — without the aid of binoculars, field guides or maps? Maybe we need to take a leaf from the approach of John Clare, as expressed in his sonnet 'Emmonsailes Heath in Winter':

I love to see the old heaths withered brake
Mingle its crimpled leaves with furze and ling

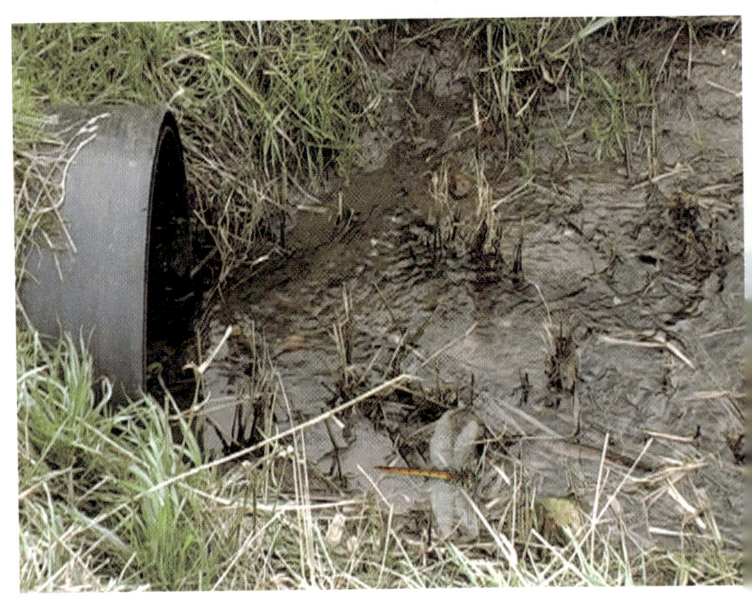

Species   **Norfolk Hawker Dragonfly,** *Aeshna Isosceles*
Location   **Tydd St Giles Fen, 2005**
Rarity   *RDB1 Endangered*
Last seen Fens, 1980s
Restricted to Norfolk and Suffolk
Specimen   Courtesy of Bedford Museum

While the old Heron from the lonely lake
Starts slow and flaps his melancholy wing
An oddling crow in idle motions swing
On the half rotten ash trees topmost twig
Beside whose trunk the gypsy makes his bed
Up flies the bouncing woodcock from the brig
Where a black quagmire quakes beneath the tread
The fieldfare chatters in the whistling thorn
And for the awe round fields and closen rove
And coy bumbarrels twenty in a drove
Flit down the hedgerows in the frozen plain
And hang on little twigs and start again.

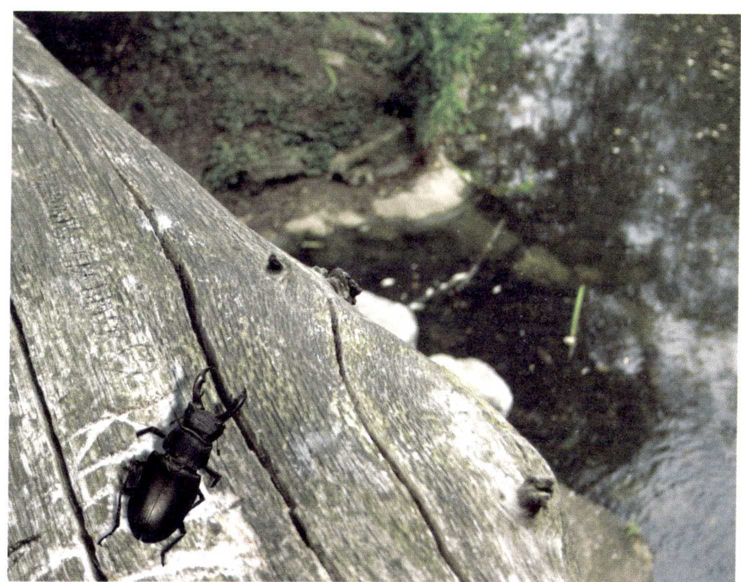

Such a simple way of viewing the landscape and its wild creatures may seem naïve to us now, but perhaps we could do with recapturing that sense of innocent wonder.

Stephen Moss is an author, broadcaster and television producer, based at the BBC Natural History Unit in Bristol, where his credits include *Birding with Bill Oddie*, *Springwatch*, and the forthcoming landmark series *The Nature of Britain*. He has written many books, including *A Bird in the Bush: a Social History of Birdwatching*.

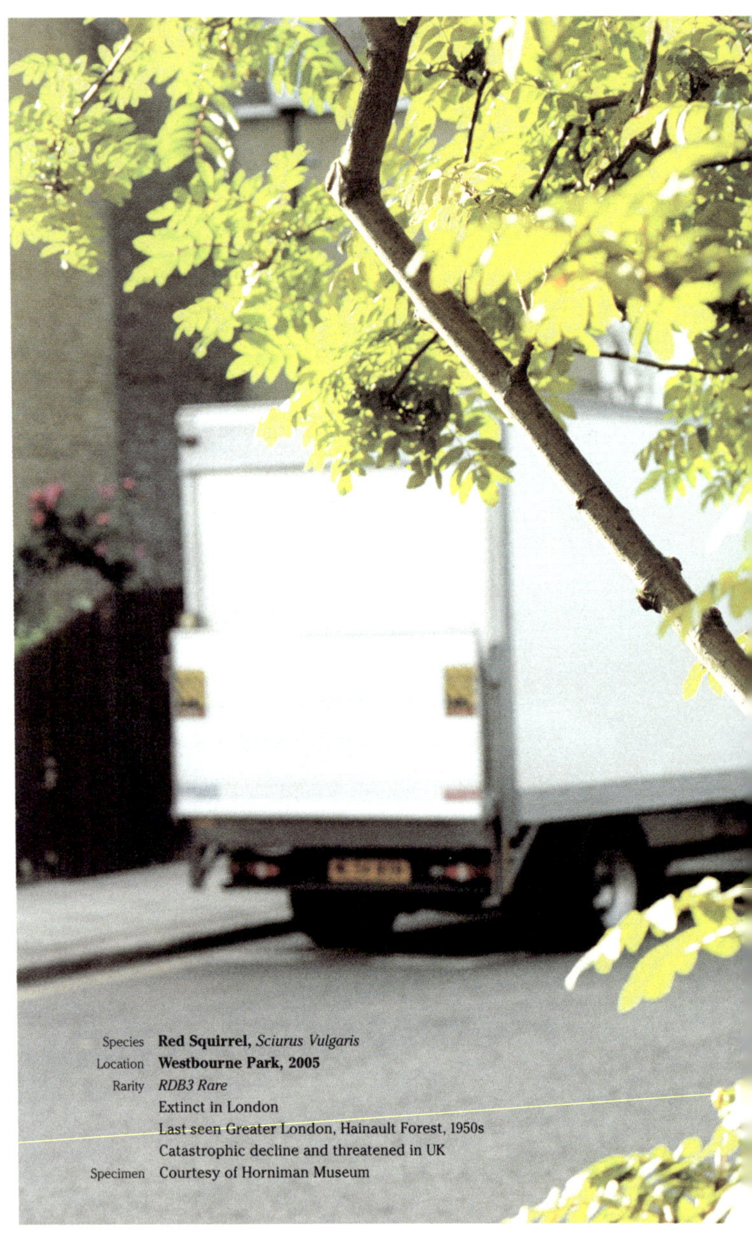

Species   **Red Squirrel,** *Sciurus Vulgaris*
Location   **Westbourne Park, 2005**
Rarity   *RDB3 Rare*
Extinct in London
Last seen Greater London, Hainault Forest, 1950s
Catastrophic decline and threatened in UK
Specimen   Courtesy of Horniman Museum

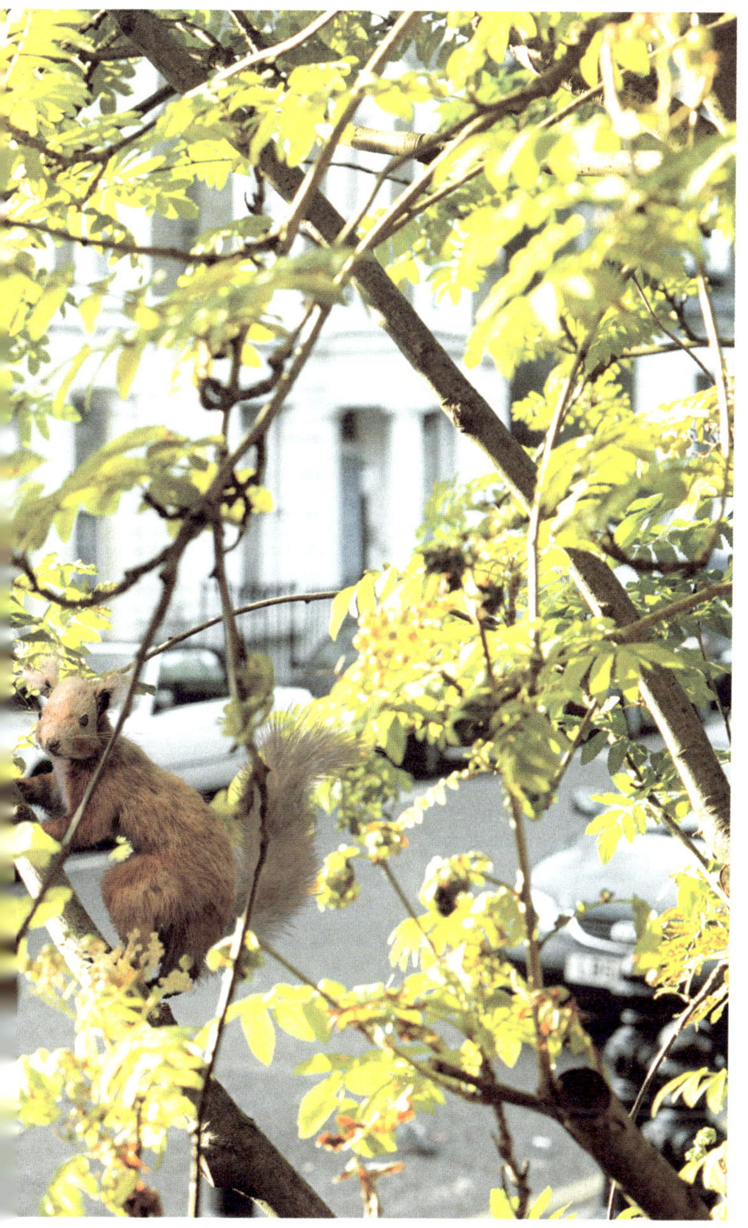

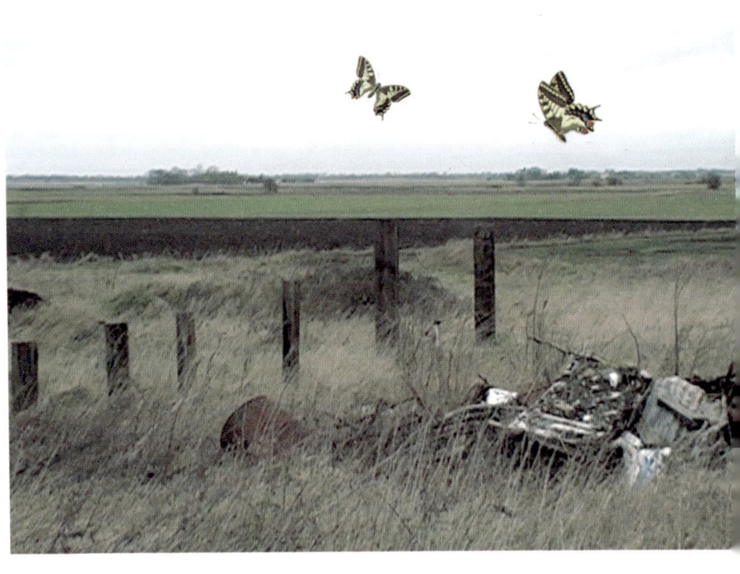

Species **Swallowtail Butterfly,** *Papilio Machaon Britannicus*
Location **Tick Fen, 2005**
Rarity *Species of Conservation Concern*; Restricted to Norfolk Broads
Native species last seen Fens, 1950
Specimen Courtesy of Bedford Museum

...and Other Stories
Nicky Coutts

Dante Alighieri had visions of birds in *paradise*. He imagined them 'like letters in the sky', fluttering slithers of a language always in formation. Inversely, he saw the depletion of birds, the repression of their speech, flight and song, as symptomatic of a descent into the circles of hell. A birdless world was Dante's nightmare and disaster, a place where nebulous joys and freedoms are suppressed and extinguished. In her essay 'Writing, Women and Birds', Hélène Cixous cites Dante's birds when she proposes that a punitive relationship with them, and other marginal creatures such as small mammals and insects, has endured at least since biblical times, when in the Book of Leviticus they are described as untouchable, unclean. She suggests that many of these oppressions have survived into the contemporary world, and warns that 'there is a whole list of institutions, media and machines that make for the banishment of birds.' For Cixous, birds are precarious fragments of knowledge, under continuous threat in a world where more conventional forms of order and power, to which she gives the collective name 'Those Bible', intrinsically require their disappearance. If those who threaten the banishment of birds should succeed, Cixous further questions how we would continue to know of them and how it would be possible to reach their place of exile after they are gone.[1]

In a new body of work, Suky Best takes as her premise the depletion, and the threat of further decline, of bird species, small mammals, insects, plants and amphibians. Of two series, collectively titled *The Return of the Native*, the first is set in the changing landscape of the bleak, wind-ravaged East Anglian Fenlands, while the second centres on London's urban environment, with its scattered and vulnerable pockets of wildlife. Best's approach to picturing those species already lost and those in the process of becoming so – those, as Cixous indicates, who are as much endangered in terms of representation as they are physically – is to subvert the iconography of the living and bring the dead back to life. First, she has photographed extinct and endangered species in museum collections, and has then literally placed them back into images of the environments they once inhabited. Some of the works take the form of still images with the species at risk

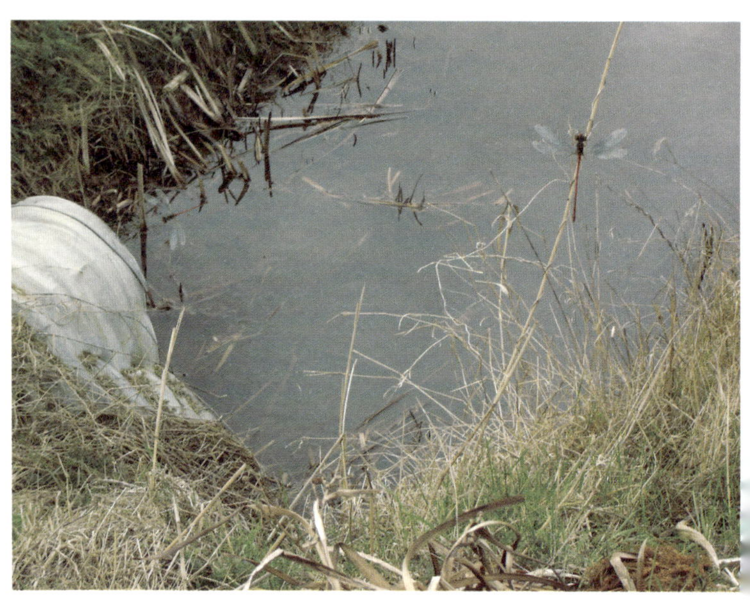

Species **Small Red Damselfly,** *Ceriagrion Tenellum*
Location **Near Thorney (Ruff Fen), 2005**
Rarity *RDB3 Rare* and nationally scarce
Last seen Fens, 1920s
Restricted to South England and West Wales
Specimen Courtesy of Bedford Museum

superimposed on its new backdrop. Others are animations, with the featured creature made to re-enact or mimic the movements of its kind.

In one of the animations, a Bearded Tit, previously well established in the Fens and now seriously endangered, clings to a slender reed in a relentless wind. It omits an odd pinging noise and flicks helplessly from side to side across the screen. At first, it seems everything is as it should be in the bird's bleak backdrop — if the man-made intrusions into its former homeland can be considered unremarkable. However, despite a theoretical seamlessness, with the native triumphantly reinstalled, there is an uneasiness to this piece, and to the body of work as a whole. Having passed through so many layers of representation, through the artist's circus of

24

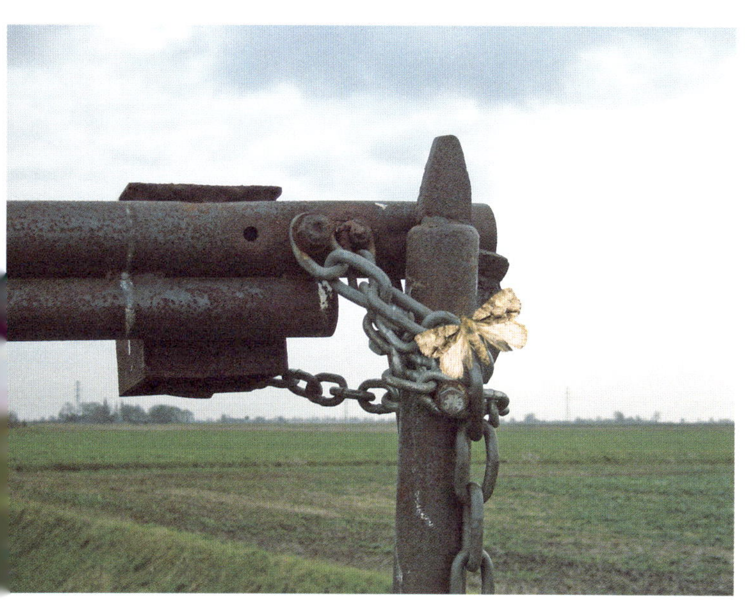

<table>
<tr><td>Species</td><td>Marsh Dagger Moth, Acronicta Strigosa</td></tr>
<tr><td>Location</td><td>Tydd St Giles Fen, 2005</td></tr>
<tr><td>Rarity</td><td>RDB3 Rare</td></tr>
<tr><td></td><td>Last seen Fens, 1939</td></tr>
<tr><td></td><td>Last sighting Rye, 1996</td></tr>
<tr><td>Specimen</td><td>Courtesy of Bedford Museum</td></tr>
</table>

mediation and illusion, it is as though this menagerie of the lost and dispossessed is pictured at the point of no return. Best's cut-and-paste make-believe world appears only to emphasise the disparity between the authority of the environments she creates, videoed in real time in the case of the animations, and the perplexing glint of artificiality which haunts the appearance of her introduced species.

Best's deliberate representation of threatened species looking at home in the contemporary world, but in a way that just falls short of being totally convincing, places her work in the company of others who have explored the properties of hoaxing and make-believe since photography's inception. Her work shares with them the hidden agenda, the story beneath the story, the blending of facts, fictions and media to create imagery that is intrinsically

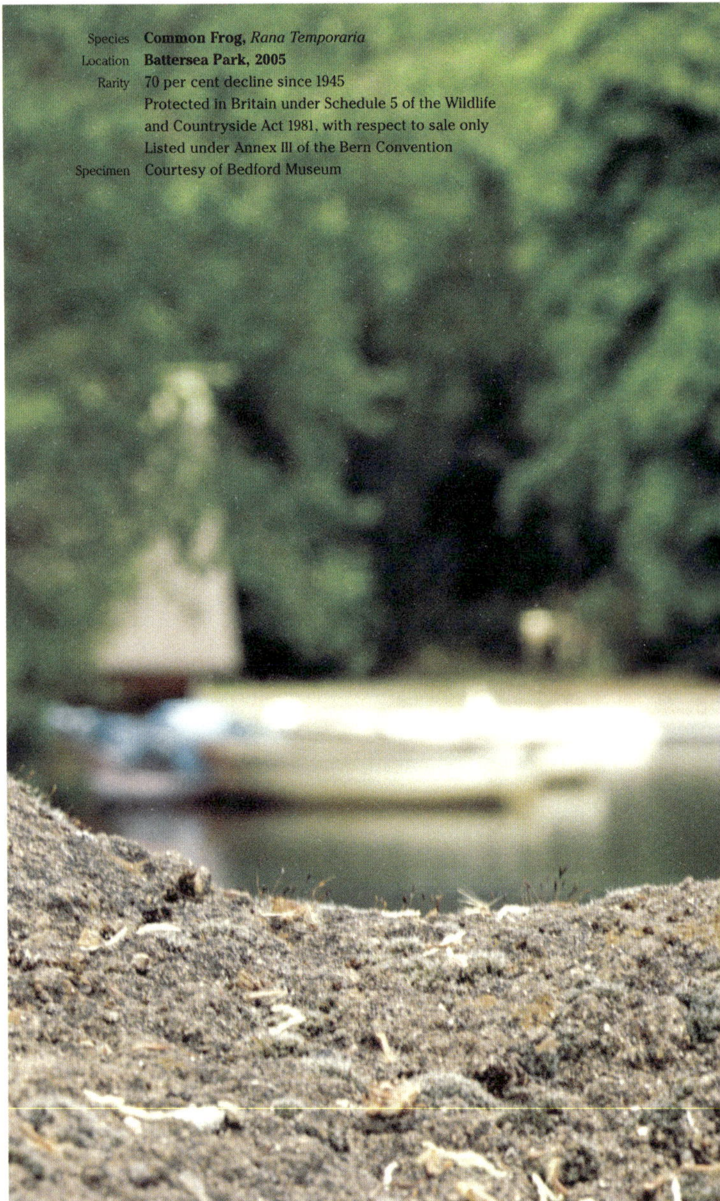

Species   Common Frog, *Rana Temporaria*
Location   Battersea Park, 2005
Rarity   70 per cent decline since 1945
           Protected in Britain under Schedule 5 of the Wildlife
           and Countryside Act 1981, with respect to sale only
           Listed under Annex III of the Bern Convention
Specimen   Courtesy of Bedford Museum

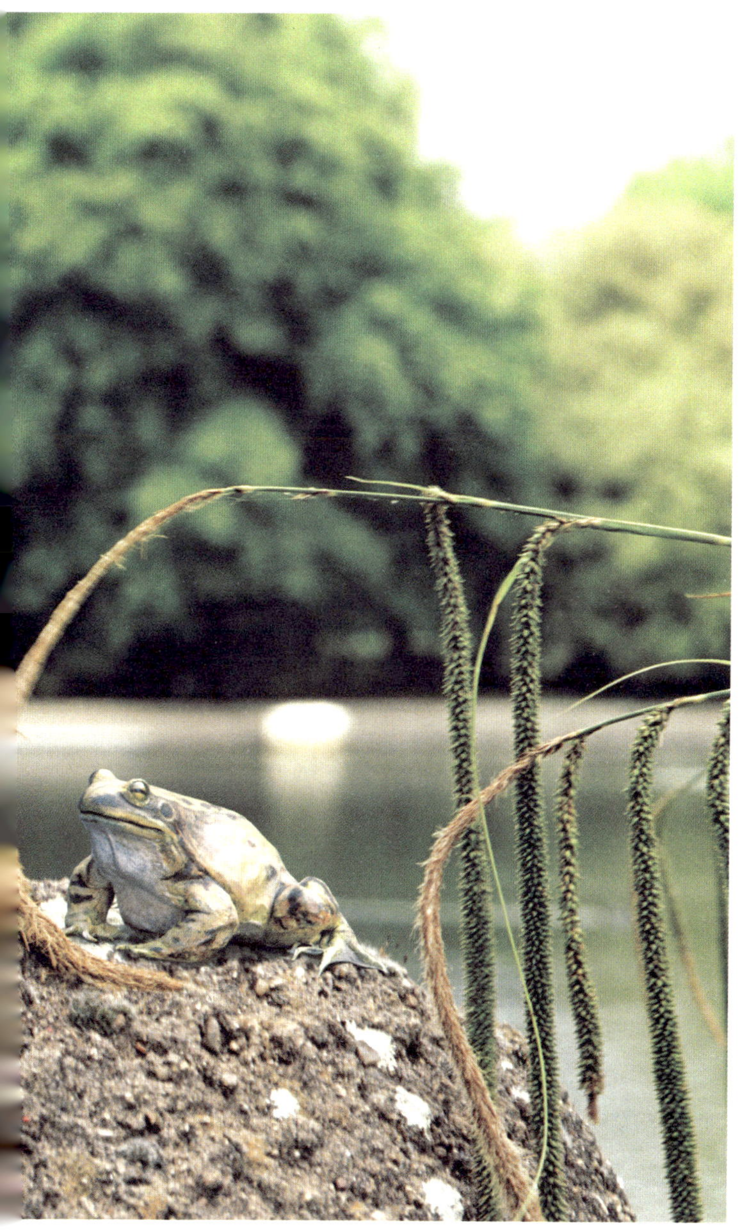

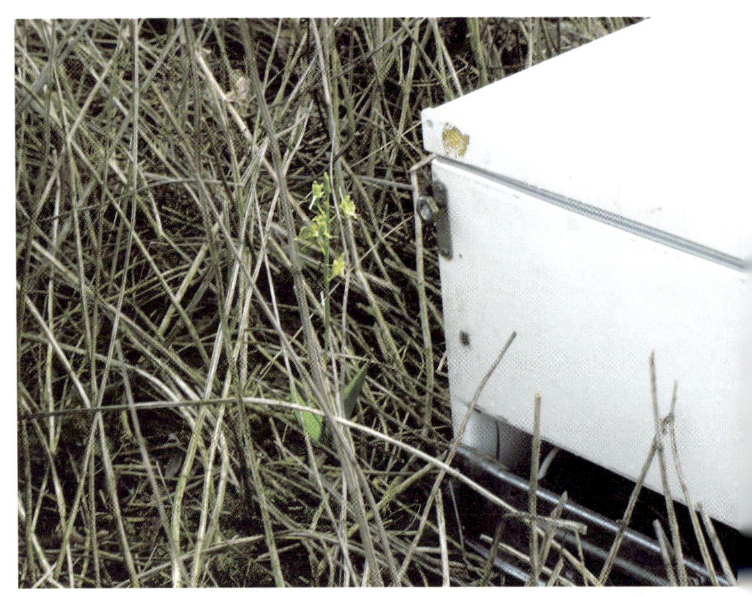

compromised. An example which has fascinated Best is the story of the Cottingley fairies, the series of photographs taken by cousins Elsie Hill and Frances Griffiths at the beginning of World War One. In a similar way to Best, they used imagery of their own contemporary environment as stage set, introduced their cobbled fairy forms and finally worked to lessen the gulf between the two, making the photographs appear as believable as they could. An astounding range of critics, theorists and photography experts of this period either wished to believe in the truth of the pictures, constructing elaborate theories that proved the potential existence of fairies in the physical world, or equally failed to reveal the nature of the girls' conspiracy. The collaborators managed to keep their secret intact for over 60 years before it subsided in a flurry of

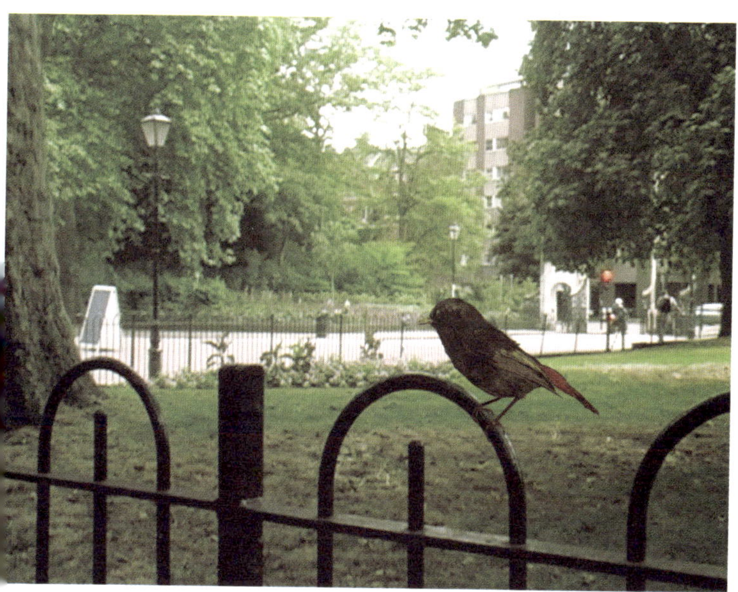

<table>
<tr><td>Species</td><td>Black Redstart, Phoenicurus Ochruros</td></tr>
<tr><td>Location</td><td>Battersea Park, 2005</td></tr>
<tr><td>Rarity</td><td>UK Birds Amber List</td></tr>
<tr><td></td><td>Under threat from development of Thames Corridor</td></tr>
<tr><td></td><td>With less than 100 pairs nesting in Britain, the Black Redstart</td></tr>
<tr><td></td><td>is a rarer British breeding bird than the Osprey or Golden Eagle</td></tr>
<tr><td>Specimen</td><td>Courtesy of Bedford Museum</td></tr>
</table>

flimsy paper and hatpins. The presence of the Great War provides a secondary form of background to the imagery. To some degree, it may indicate why such an overwhelming need to imagine such outlandish, otherworldly phenomena existed when the real world was becoming ever more violent and difficult to depend on. 'There are fairies at the bottom of the garden...' is the first line of a poem reproduced in *Punch* magazine, which was in the girls' possession at around the time the first fairy photograph was taken. It had already evolved to become a phrase used by the Royal Corps of Signals to denote the sighting of the enemy. It would seem that the magical qualities of fairylore within a threatening and destructive climate, Dante's much-loved birds which he haunted with the possibility of their own annihilation, Best's fabrication of an ideal,

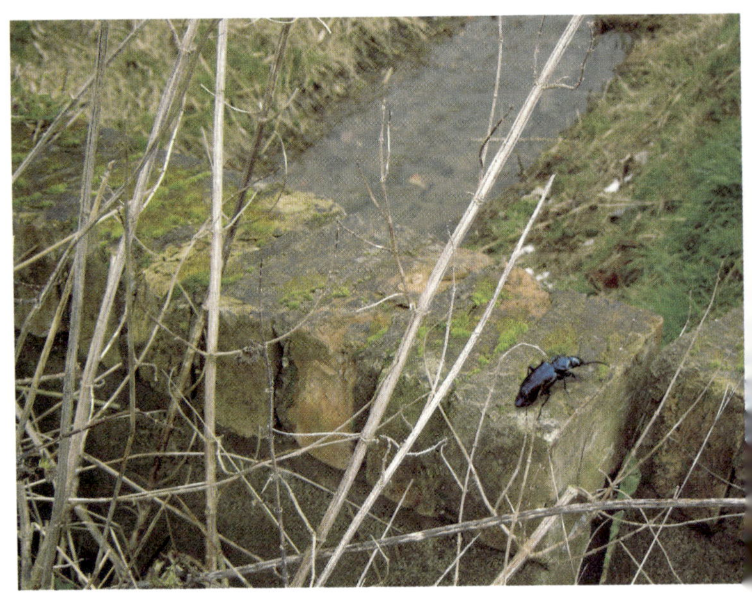

Species **Ground Beetle,** *Pterostichus Aterrimus*
Location **Near Crowland, 2005**
Rarity *RDB1 Endangered*
Extinct in Britain since 1973
Last seen Fens early 20th century
Specimen image Courtesy of Dr Roy Anderson

complete nature at a time when many of the species she represents
are already beyond her grasp — all indicate the ability of hoaxing
and make-believe to simultaneously veil and reveal troubling
realities which are otherwise difficult to reach.

'Fauna', a more recent hoax by Joan Fontcuberta and Pere
Formiguera, shares with Best's work the intention of multiplying
the variety of creatures in the current environment through
constructing layers of fiction. From 1986-88, the artists purported
to work with a fictitious natural scientist, Dr Amiesenhaufen, who
constructed hybrid animals from the body parts of recently
deceased zoo animals and presented them as 'found' creatures
in an attempt to prove an alternative to currently held views on
evolution. After documenting these collated creatures, the artists

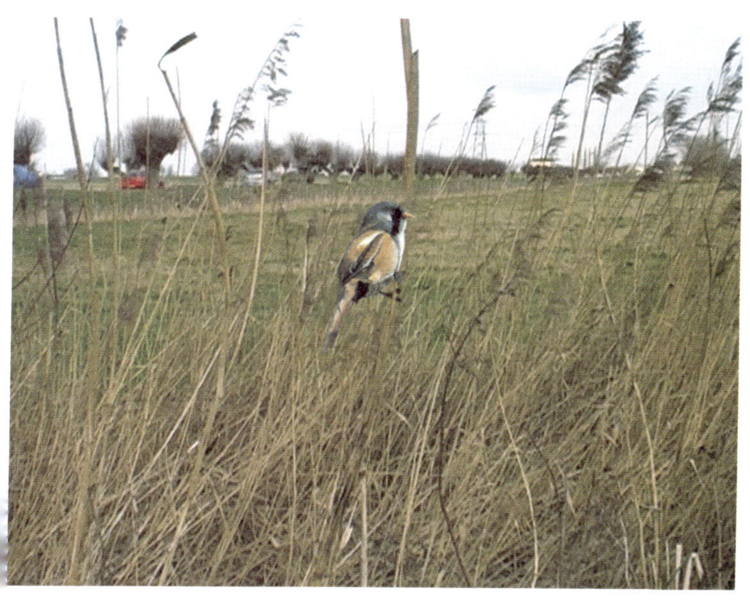

<table>
<tr><td>Species</td><td>Bearded Tit, Panurus Biarmicus</td></tr>
<tr><td>Location</td><td>Whittlesey, 2005</td></tr>
<tr><td>Rarity</td><td>UK Birds Amber List
Previously widespread on Fens
Hope for breeding pairs to return to Wicken Fen,
Woodwalton and Needingworth Quarry</td></tr>
<tr><td>Specimen image</td><td>Courtesy of RSPB</td></tr>
</table>

placed their material in museums and institutions replicating the conventional displays of zoology. In a poll conducted by one of the museums' education departments, 30 per cent of visitors aged between 20 and 30 believed that some of the creatures could actually have existed. Fontcuberta remarks in an interview with Diane Neumaier in 1991:'I am talking about flying elephants, hairy snakes or snakes with twelve chicken legs, rats with snake tails, things like that.' That their creations should have proved so credible clearly astounds Fontcuberta, despite the fact that their believability is central to his and Formiguera's work. Fontcuberta, like Best, appears to recognise, and subvert to his own ends, the power of Cixous' 'Those Bible', the entities that legitimise certain forms of knowledge over those that it considers more marginal.

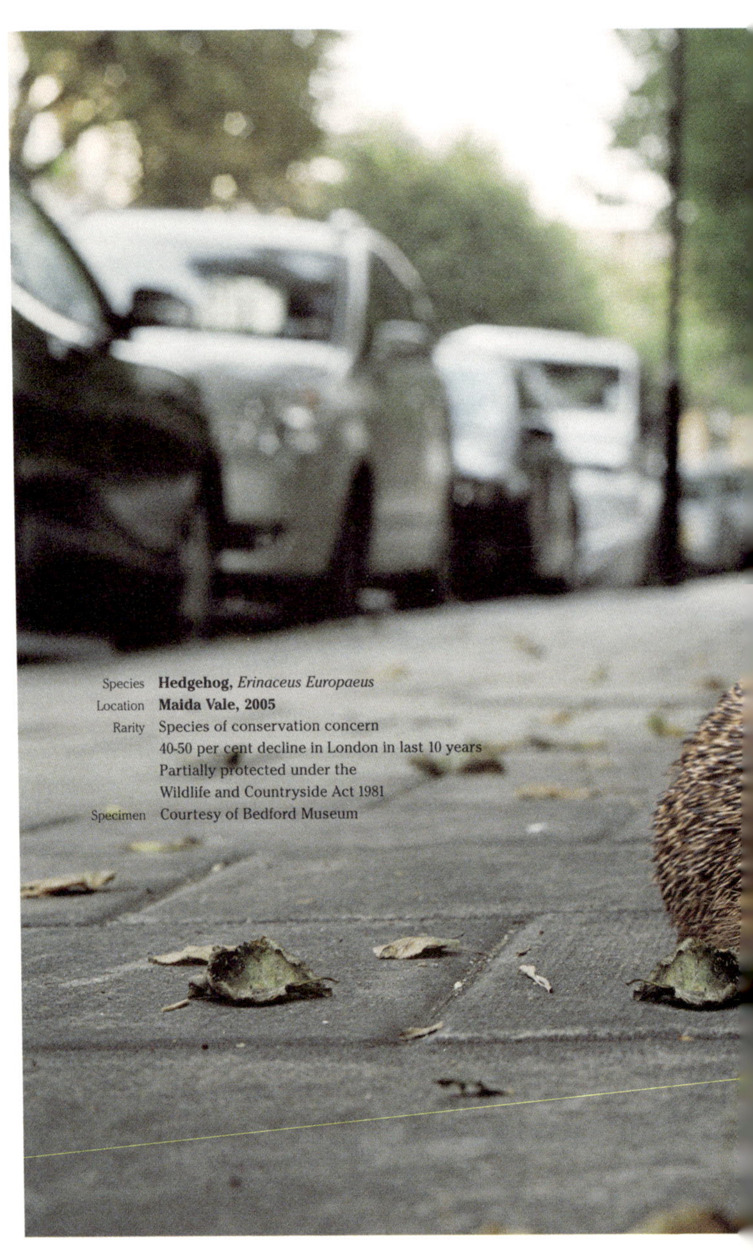
Species   Hedgehog, *Erinaceus Europaeus*
Location   Maida Vale, 2005
Rarity   Species of conservation concern
40-50 per cent decline in London in last 10 years
Partially protected under the
Wildlife and Countryside Act 1981
Specimen   Courtesy of Bedford Museum

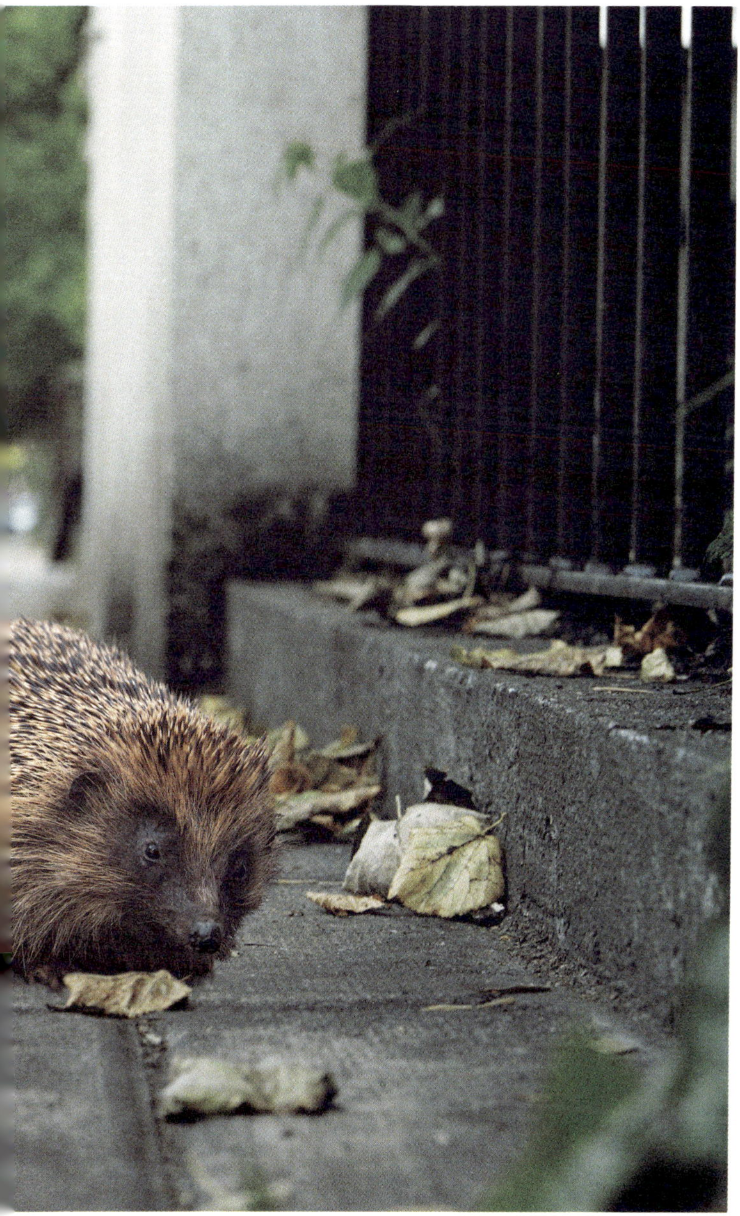

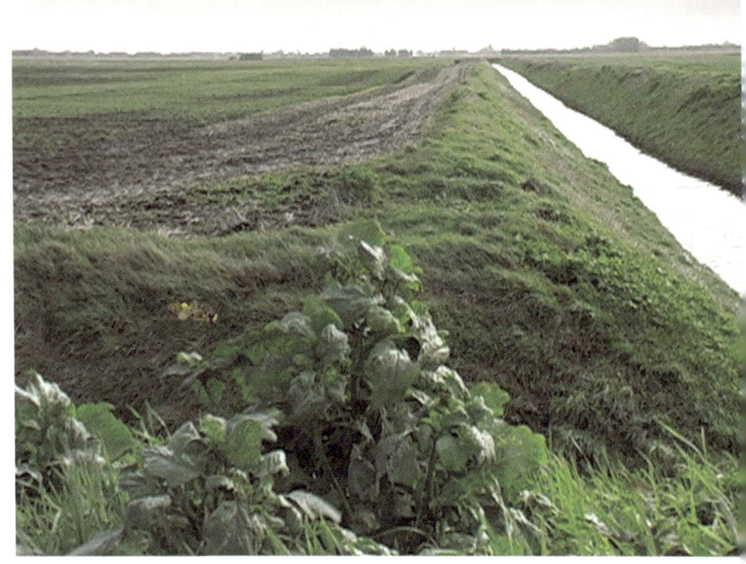

Species **Soldier Fly,** *Stratiomys Chamaeleon*
Location **Near Murrow, 2005**
Rarity *RDB1 Endangered*
Present at Wicken Fen but otherwise lost to the Fens since 1990s
Specimen image Courtesy of Hans VR

Speaking of the siting of his work in museums, Fontcuberta concedes: 'We need to believe and to feel ourselves safe inside these institutions, because somehow our knowledge is based on the respect we feel for them.' It is this safety in an inherited, but not inherent, type of knowledge that Fontcuberta and Best seek to unravel. Their success depends on the precision they apply to the hoax. For both, to make their menageries too convincing in their new environments would be to threaten them with complete disappearance. To make them not convincing enough would be to encourage an atmosphere of comedy to overwhelm the work. If the reassignment of knowledge is not precise enough, Best's assortment of marginal creatures, in particular, runs the risk of itself being open to accusations of marginalisation. [2]

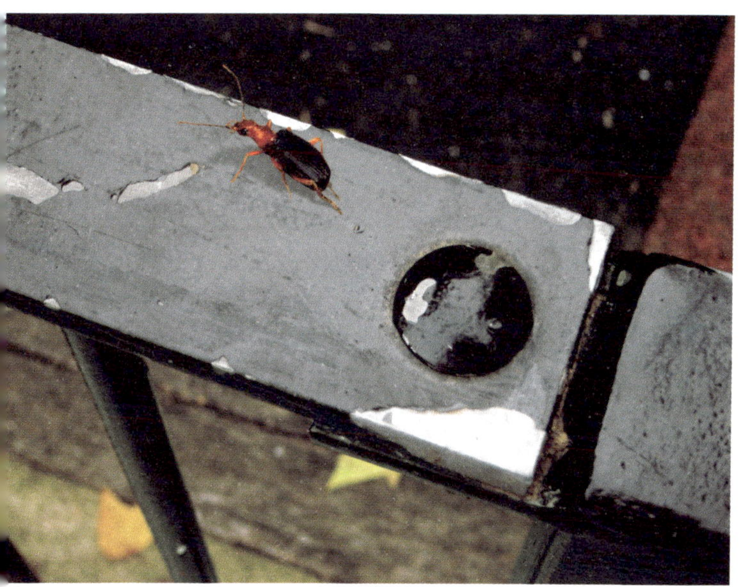

In one of Best's still images, a Bombardier Beetle is pictured wandering ponderously along some railings. This insect, rare and in decline in London and scarce in the rest of the UK, swells up and explodes a noxious cocktail of foul-smelling gases in the direction of its enemies whenever it feels threatened. As though paralleling Fontcuberta's fictions with extraordinary facts, its behaviour has been used by creationists in an attempt to disprove dominant theories of evolution. In another of Best's animations, a Nightingale sings plaintively in the dusk near Battersea Bridge, while people wander past, oblivious. The Nightingale, declining throughout the UK, has nearly 220 song types. A German study of these birds next to roads found that they had to sing at around 93 decibels to be heard over the morning rush hour traffic: a level of

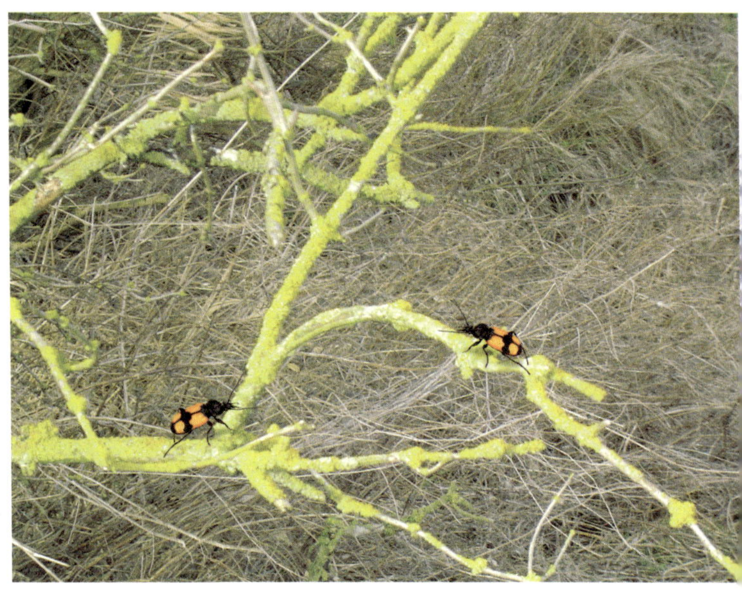

sound equivalent to having your ear close to a motorcycle exhaust at full power.

Dante's extreme vision of a world without birds may hover as a distant reality. Cixous' concerns, however, at the waning of the natural world and our inability to know what to do with or without the mysterious, idiosyncratic, seemingly inconsequential knowledge we encounter when we observe the habits of creatures facing extinction, seem very imminent indeed. Through the body of work *The Return of the Native*, Best examines this dilemma and seems to ask how we will continue to know of extinct species and how it will be possible to reach their place of exile after they are gone.

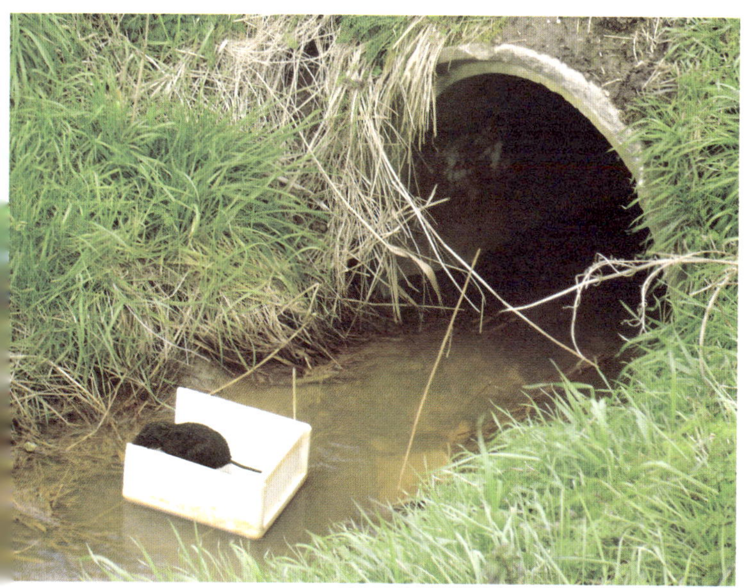

Species **Water Vole,** *Arvicola Terrestris*
Location **Whaplode St Catherine, 2005**
Rarity Partially protected under Schedule 5 of the
Wildlife and Countryside Act 1981
Scarce in Fens after catastrophic decline nationally this century
Specimen Courtesy of Bedford Museum

1 *Animal Philosophy, Ethics and Identity*, ed. M. Calarco & P. Atterton,
London & NY: Continuum, 2004, p.171

2 *Art and Photography*, ed. D. Campany, Phaidon: London, 2003, p.284

Other References

The Divine Comedy, Dante Alighieri, trans. H. Longfellow London: Routledge, 1904

Fairies, The Cottingley Photographs and their Sequel, E. Gardner,
The Theosophical Publishing House London Ltd., 1945

The Case of the Cottingley Fairies, J. Cooper, London: Robert Hale, 1990

Postmodernism and the Environmental Crisis, Arran E. Gare, London & NY:
Routledge, 1995

Nicky Coutts is an artist, writer and Fine Art Fellow at Middlesex University

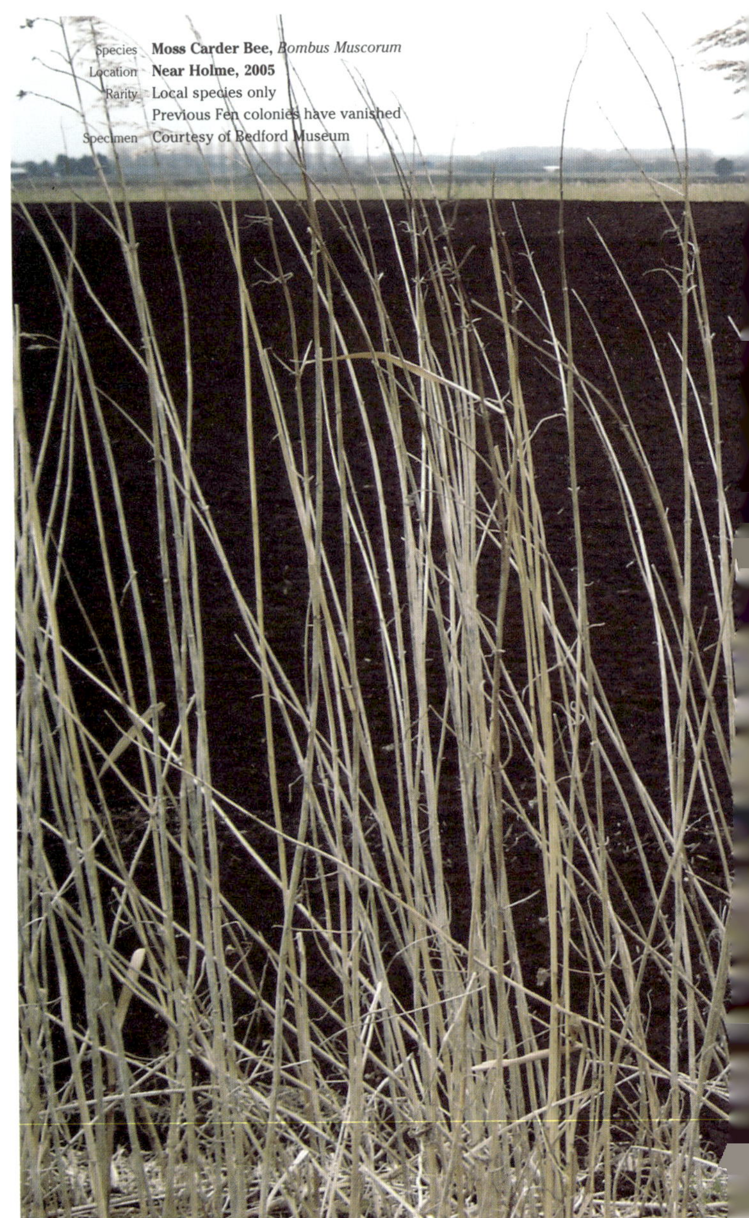

Species   **Moss Carder Bee,** *Bombus Muscorum*
Location   **Near Holme, 2005**
Rarity   Local species only
Previous Fen colonies have vanished
Specimen   Courtesy of Bedford Museum

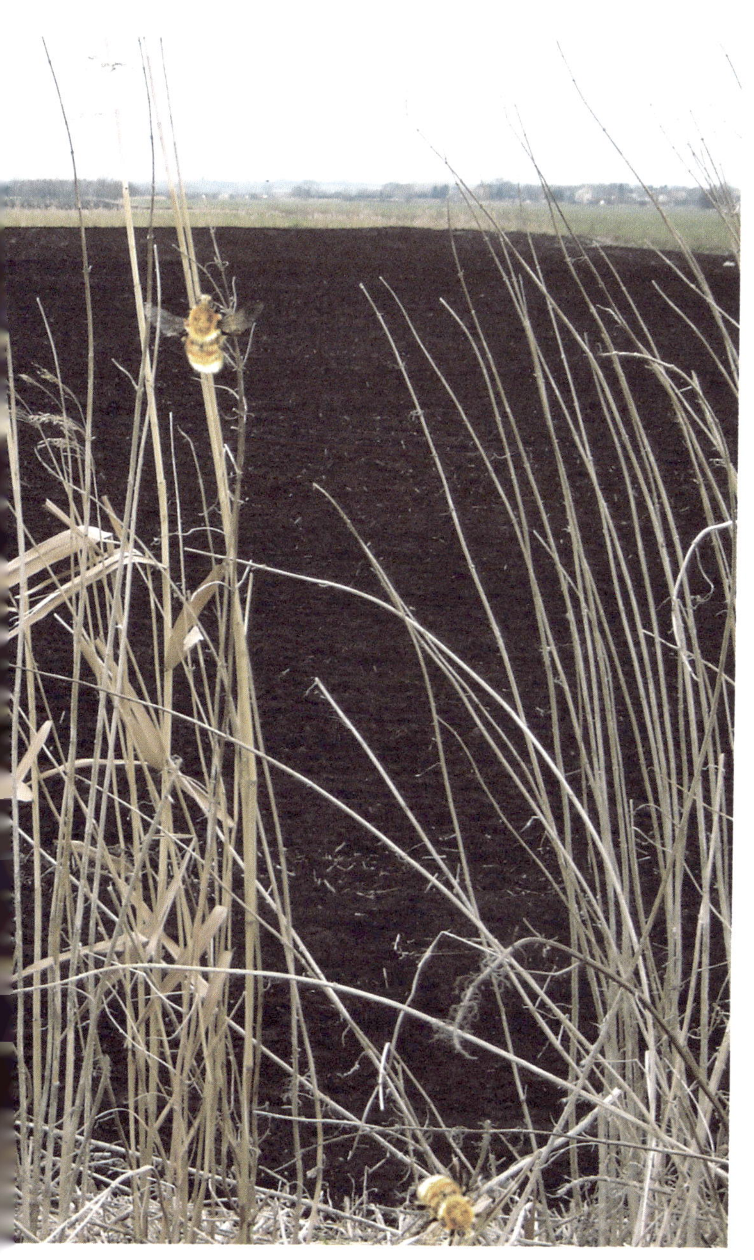

Conservation Categories

**The World Conservation Union (IUCN)
Red List of Threatened Species**

www.iucnredlist.org is a comprehensive inventory of the global
conservation status of plant and animal species. The lists provide
a baseline for guiding conservation decisions of governments,
NGO's and other institutions. They are one element used to inform
and revise the UK Biodiversity Action Plans.

There are two main goals of the IUCN, which are to:

- Identify and document those species most in need of
  conservation attention if global extinction rates are to be reduced

- Provide a global index of the state of degeneration of biodiversity

Species are categorised according to evidence available and are
given a taxon dependent on a series of criteria including population
size, population depletion or geographic range of the species and
the risk of extinction in the wild.

The following categories may be seen in these works:

Extinct / Extinct in the Wild — where the last individual has
died or the species survives only in cultivation, in captivity or as
a naturalised population well outside the past range.

RDB1 Endangered — considered to be facing a very high risk
of extinction in the wild.

RDB2 Vulnerable — considered to be facing a high risk of
extinction in the wild.

RDB3 Rare / Near Threatened — not immediately threatened
but close to qualifying for, or likely to qualify for, a threatened
category in the future.

Notable Species

In the UK, a number of species are also listed as **Notable**, where
they do not have RDB status but where there is a conservation
concern because of scarcity.

UK Birds Red List — High Conservation Concern

With more than 50 per cent decline in UK breeding population
over the last 25 years, the Marsh Warbler and House Sparrow
(more than 70 per cent decline in London) are included as two
of the 40 Red-listed birds.

UK Birds Amber List — Medium Conservation Concern

With localised breeding sites, low breeding population and
moderate population decline respectively, the Bearded Tit, Black
Redstart and Nightingale are three of 121 Amber-listed birds.

Butterfly and Moth Listings

In the UK, listed categories are **Priority Species** or **Species of
Conservation Concern**. Species are listed when they are globally
threatened, or the UK has more than 25 per cent of the total world
population, or where numbers have declined by more than 25 per
cent in the last 25 years, or where it is listed under international
legislation.

It should be noted that a number of species in these works were
previously very common and as a consequence there may not
be historical records or data to give accurate rates of decline, such
as for the Common Frog.

Image Locations

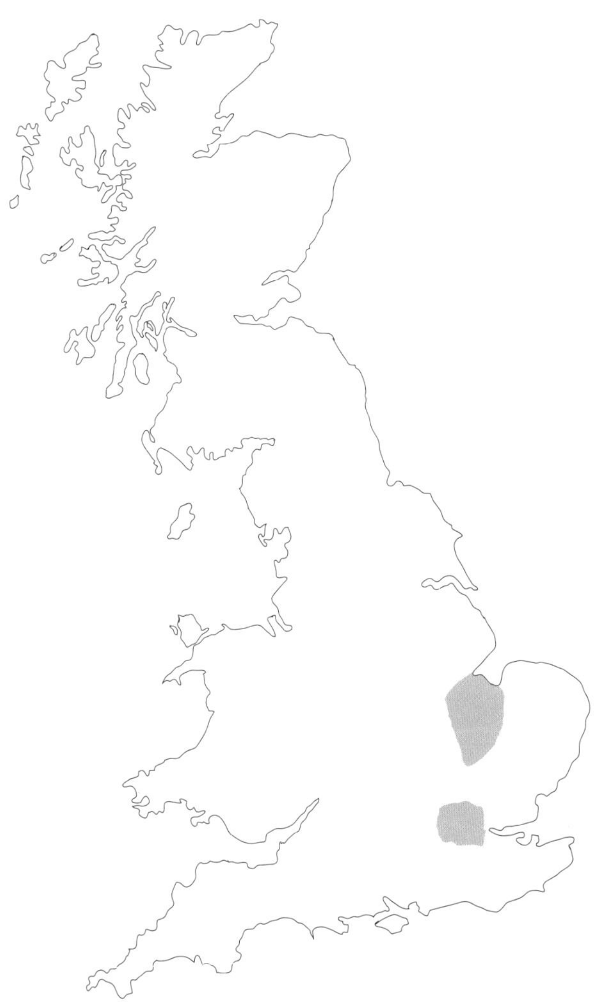

Index

Suky Best

Lives and works in London
MA Photography, Royal College of Art, 1992-95
BSc (Hons) Geography, North London Polytechnic, 1981-84

Selected Solo Exhibitions

2005 *The Return of the Native* BCA Gallery, Bedford;
Pump House Gallery, London
Wild West (in collaboration with Rory Hamilton),
Danielle Arnaud Contemporary Art, London

2002 *Recent Work* Danielle Arnaud Contemporary Art, London

2001 *10 Journeys* Dartmoor Insight / Aha / DA2
Commission and tour
the way we live now Lighthouse Media Gallery,
Wolverhampton

2000 *Walking Meditation* Cleeve Abbey, Somerset
the time for talking is over Margaret Harvey Gallery, St Albans

1999 *Photo-Love 2* Amsterdam Centrum voor Fotographie

1997 *That was then...This is now!* The Photographers' Gallery,
London

Selected Group Exhibitions

2005 *ArtNow Lightbox* Tate Britain, London
The Projection Room County Hall, Dun Laoghaire, Eire

2004 *Magic within Reason* Domo Ball Gallery, London
Trace Edition Hirschl Contemporary Art, London

2003 *Exhumed* The Museum of Garden History, London

2002 *Winners' Exhibition John Kobal 10th Anniversary*
National Portrait Gallery, London
Julian Walker and Suky Best Unit 2, London

2000 *East International* Norwich Gallery
ex-machina Neue Gesellschaft für Bildende Kunst, Berlin

1999 *The 23rd International Biennial of Graphic Art*
Ljubljana, Slovenia

1998 *The Fotonovela* Camerawork, San Francisco

1997 *Public Relations: New British Photography*, Stadthaus,
Ulm, Germany
dislocations Northern Photographic Triennial, Oulu, Finland

Awards

2004 Wellcome Trust SCIART Research and Development award
2002 London Arts Board Individual Artist award
2000 Year of the Artist residency, Cleeve Abbey, funded by
         DA2, English Heritage and South West Arts
1998 Two-year Fellowship in Printmaking, University of
         Wolverhampton, funded by the Henry Moore Foundation
1994 John Kobal Photographic Portrait Award, Joint First Prize

Solo Publications

2005 *The Return of the Native*, Steven Bode (Ed.),
         Film and Video Umbrella
2001 *the time for talking is over*, Matthew Shaul (Ed.),
         University of Hertfordshire
1999 *Suky Best presents These are Restless Times: a Short
         Moving Picture*, Women's Art Library
1997 *Photo-Love Vol. 3, Suky Best presents Dorigen's Promise*,
         Festerman Press
         *Photo-Love Vol. 2, Suky Best presents That was then...
         This is now!*, Festerman Press
1995 *Photo-Love Vol. 1, Suky Best presents*, Festerman Press

Suky Best would like to thank:

Elizabeth Robin for researching all the species of birds, mammals and insects for this project and for sourcing sounds, specimens and images

Nicky Coutts and Stephen Moss for their essays

Chris Andrew for access to the Natural History Collection, Bedford Museum

Jim Brock and Jo Hatton of the Horniman Museum, London

John Cleur and Ross Davenport of Goldenshot Digital

The British Library Sound Archive

The wildlife photographers who gave permission for image use:
Dr Roy Anderson, Roger Key, Hans VR, Harri Arkkio, RSPB, Alan Tate,
Paul Chesterfield and Jayne Herbert (Cornwall Wildlife)

Mike Jones, Steven Bode, Caroline Smith, Nina Ernst and everyone at
Film and Video Umbrella

Katie Walton, Laura Pottinger, Hedj Ijyaho-Dollman and Susannah Oliver at
BCA Gallery, Bedford

Nick Kaplony, Sandra Ross and Susie Gray at Pump House Gallery, London

Simon Willmoth and Norwich School of Art and Design

David Moore for his assistance with the production of the London backgrounds
and larger animal images

Ben Bocquelet, Annie Cattrell, Jo Chiles, Rory Hamilton, Marion Kalmus,
Ren Pesci and Kimo Morrison for their help with this project

The Return of the Native Suky Best

Published by Film and Video Umbrella

Edited by Steven Bode, Editorial Assistance from Nina Ernst
Designed by Richard Bonner-Morgan, Printed by Trichrom Ltd

Published on the occasion of the exhibition *The Return of the Native*
at Pump House Gallery, London, 26 October – 19 December 2005
First exhibited at BCA Gallery, Bedford, 23 April – 4 June 2005

Publication supported by Arts Council England

Printed in an edition of 500
ISBN 1-90427-020-4
© 2005, Film and Video Umbrella, the artist and the authors

Film and Video Umbrella
52 Bermondsey Street, London SE1 3UD
T 020 7407 7755 F 020 7407 7766
E info@fvu.co.uk W www.fvumbrella.com

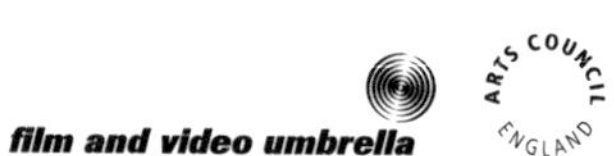

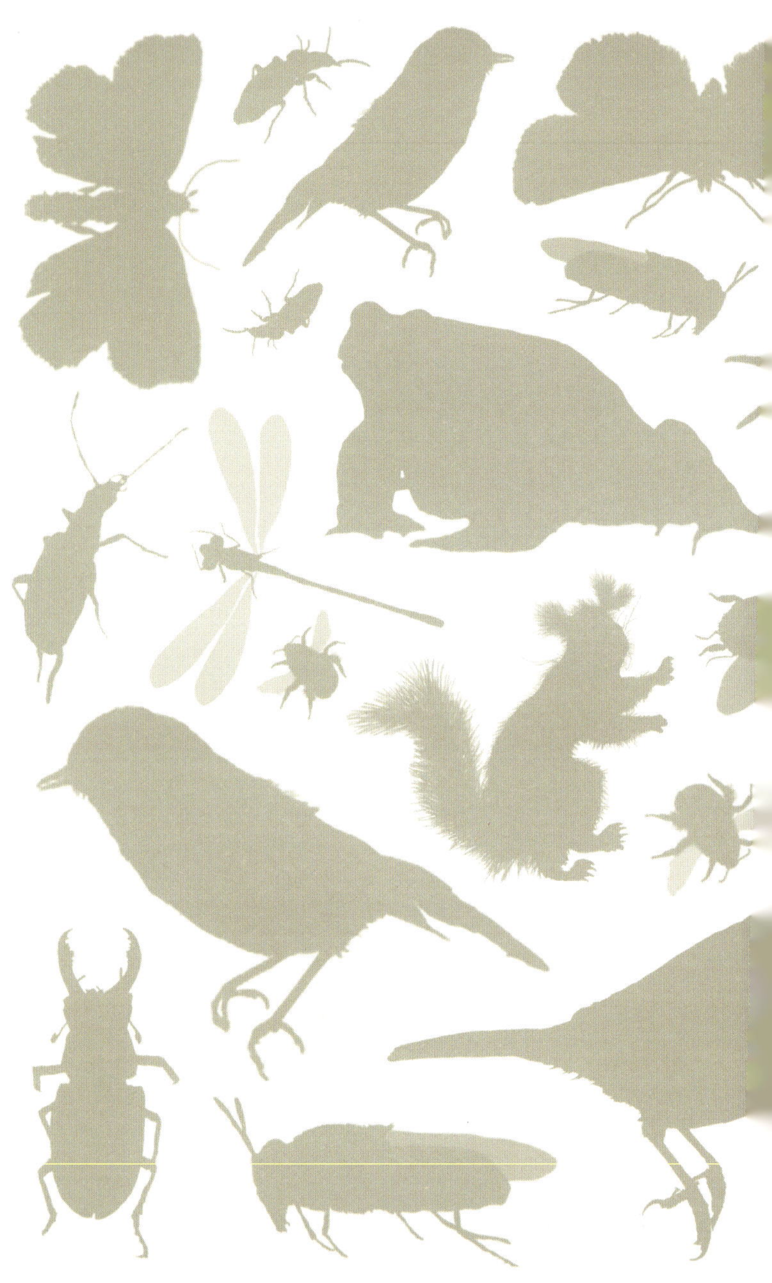